Reptile World

# Snapping Turtles

by Cari Meister

Bullfrog
Books

Reader

## Ideas for Parents and Teachers

Bullfrog Books let children practice reading informational text at the earliest reading levels. Repetition, familiar words, and photo labels support early readers.

### Before Reading
• Discuss the cover photo. What does it tell them?

• Look at the picture glossary together. Read and discuss the words.

### Read the Book
• "Walk" through the book and look at the photos. Let the child ask questions. Point out the photo labels.

• Read the book to the child, or have him or her read independently.

### After Reading
• Prompt the child to think more. Ask: Have you ever seen a snapping turtle? Did you see it open its mouth?

Bullfrog Books are published by Jump!
5357 Penn Avenue South
Minneapolis, MN 55419
www.jumplibrary.com

Library of Congress Cataloging-in-Publication Data

Meister, Cari, author.
 Snapping turtles / by Cari Meister.
   pages cm. — (Reptile world)
 "Bullfrog Books are published by Jump!."
 Summary: "This photo-illustrated book for beginning readers describes the physical features and behaviors of snapping turtles. Includes picture glossary and index"— Provided by publisher.
 Audience: 5–8.
 Audience: K to grade 3.
 Includes index.
 ISBN 978-1-62031-199-8 (hardcover: alk. paper) —
 ISBN 978-1-62496-286-8 (ebook)
 1. Snapping turtles—Juvenile literature.  I. Title.
 QL666.C539M45 2015
 597.92'2—dc23

 2014043358

Series Editor: Jenny Fretland VanVoorst
Series Designer: Ellen Huber
Book Designer: Michelle Sonnek
Photo Researcher: Michelle Sonnek

Photo Credits: All photos by Shutterstock except: Alamy, 3, 19; Andrew Williams/Critter Zone, 12–13; ardea, 14–15, 23tr; Biosphoto, 5; Corbis, cover, 9; Getty, 4, 6, 22, 23bl; National Geographic Creative, 10–11, 23tl; Nature Picture Library, 8; Science Source, 12, 23br; Shutterstock, 1, 18, 24; SuperStock, 6–7, 16–17; Visuals Unlimited, 20–21.

Printed in the United States of America at Corporate Graphics in North Mankato, Minnesota.

# Table of Contents

# Strong Jaws

It is night.
A snapping turtle hunts.

Snap!

He grabs a snake.

Now he dives.

He sits on the pond floor.

He waits.

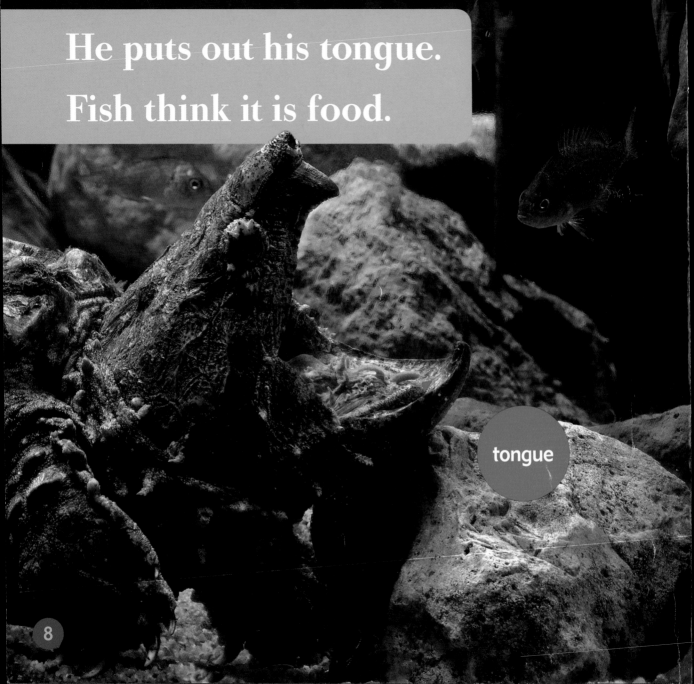

He puts out his tongue.
Fish think it is food.

tongue

They come.

Snap!

beak

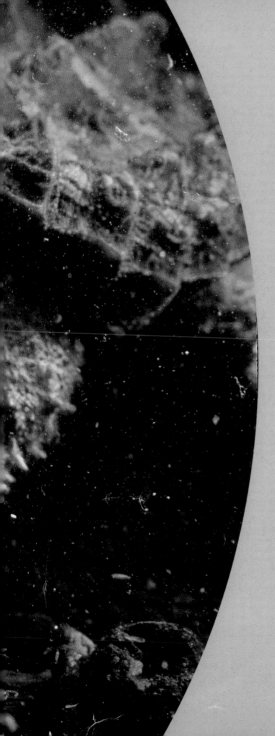

His beak is sharp.

His jaws are strong.

He eats.

Baby snappers
hatch from eggs.

They go to
the water
right away.

eggs

Some do not make it.

Birds eat them.

Fish eat them.

Big snappers do not
have enemies.

Animals stay away
from them.

They are too fierce.

They have sharp claws.

They have thick shells.
They bite.

They can live
a long time.

Some live to be
70 years old!

# Parts of a Snapping Turtle

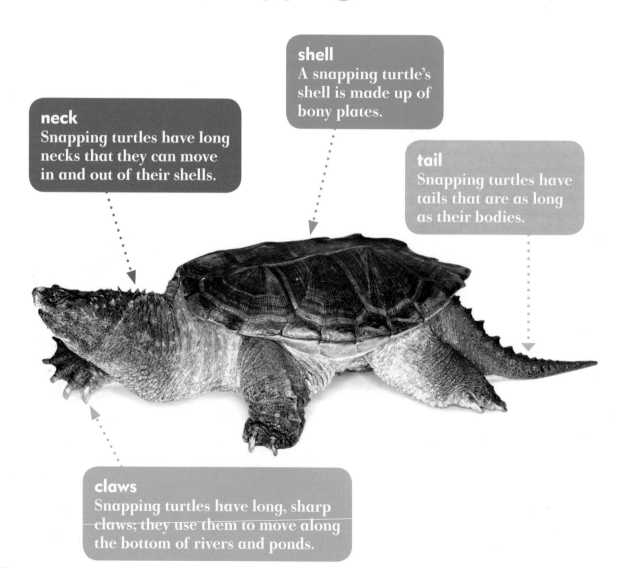

**shell**
A snapping turtle's shell is made up of bony plates.

**neck**
Snapping turtles have long necks that they can move in and out of their shells.

**tail**
Snapping turtles have tails that are as long as their bodies.

**claws**
Snapping turtles have long, sharp claws; they use them to move along the bottom of rivers and ponds.

# Picture Glossary

**beak**
The hard, horny parts of a snapping turtle's mouth.

**enemies**
Other animals that want to eat or hurt snapping turtles.

**dive**
To go headfirst into water.

**hatch**
To be born from an egg.

# Index

# To Learn More

Learning more is as easy as 1, 2, 3.

1) Go to www.factsurfer.com

2) Enter "snappingturtles" into the search box.

3) Click the "Surf" button to see a list of websites.

With factsurfer.com, finding more information is just a click away.